DEAR AZULA, I HAVE A CRUSH ON DANNY PHANTOM

DEAR AZULA,
I HAVE A CRUSH ON
DANNY PHANTOM

poems by

Jackson Neal and Azura Tyabji

◇

Published by Button Poetry / Exploding Pinecone Press
Minneapolis, MN 55403 | http://www.buttonpoetry.com

CONTENTS

DEAR AZULA,
I HAVE A CRUSH ON
DANNY PHANTOM

SELF PORTRAIT: DANNY PHANTOM

I enter the portal young, unfamiliar with love or
    what it looks like. In the algorithm,
        in gay porn,
           in the hole of my eye

gaped wide two boys   slurp each other's shadows.
    Strobe light lovers
        animating the animal inside. The neon iris

    of a crocodile, its pupil slashed
        into an entry. I enter night
           every night, a nasty emerald.

Green light crusts my eyes while I run
    the simulation again: again: again:
        crooked limbs thrashed across the black slop oculus.

    Swimming grim & glossy in vixen pixels,
        a string of code wraps around my throat,
           gawking at what two men can do.

One, elbow deep in another
    digit fiction. What some call parasite
        I call practice. Pressing two bodies

    into one, slashing them apart.
        Pythons sprouting second heads.
           My face multiplying in the mirror

I am the exploded lover &
    the boy who breaks him open &
    the guilty black glass &
    the scared child looking back
    asking what this means about me.
    what I could be.

Look at me,
I'm flickering.
I'm ghost-boy one & ghost-boy two.

Now tell me who is who.

I HAVE A CRUSH ON SHEGO
Kim Possible

Chlorosis /noun/ – [klə-'rō-səs]
   a. Loss of the green color in iron-deficient plants
   b. (19th cent.) Sickness as a result of unrequited love, resulting
      in an anemic, green complexion

I am twelve and just learned how to lock my door.
The evening is young, ripe with reruns.
My clothes and personality have grown
unflattering overnight, so I cut

my tights into a bodysuit and blush
green. Disney Channel past 9 p.m. is a rite
aglow with agency, flushed with the strain
of longing I only know to call a fever.

If Buttercup of the Powerpuff Girls
is my first preteen permission to be edgy,
you herald a fist I will pray for.
She-go,

ode to pursed lips after bared teeth. Song for me
to revel in alone. My emerald blueprint of cunning.
So glamorous, it almost doesn't matter that
no one seems to love you back.

You pin Kim to the banquet table,
chandelier above you glittering like a million keys, a tension
that seems to stretch forever, until it doesn't.

I understand why you choose to keep fighting her.
I would too, if it meant our wrists could stay that close.

I am lime feverish with want.
There is a name for this villainy I have yet to know.

I am twelve, and know girls don't hold other girls
beyond friendship and rivalry, but I love

how the men in your lives are forgettable.
I love fighting boys slick with mud after that.

I love how the girls watch me.

ZUKO'S ODE

Avatar: The Last Airbender

"you burn me" —*Sappho*

When I was a boy, I watched my father
pull the entrails from a doe,

like slipping off his clothes.
When I was a Boy

Scout, we played a game
we made ourselves, matches and Axe

body spray and a squirrel
caught in twine.

What wicked rituals make a man
into a man, and how can I perform?

Oh sunrise. Oh blasted eye.
Oh bright arrow of light,

run your blade through me.
Oh honor, oh honor.

You are a mask with my father's face.
Each night I wear you in the mirror,

and each night I watch his burn mark disappear.
Ozai. Ozai. I learned love as a willingness

to burn. A father
striking his son's

left eye into night.
So each night I balm my burn mark

imagining how I'll hurt my son.
The word "ozai" combines *fire* and *disaster*.

The word "zuko" means *failure*—
a second scar my father gave me.

Oh excellence. Oh effigy.
I am not a man. I am the creature

shame makes of men.
Oh blue fire. Oh sister dearest.

I am not a monster. I am a boy who wants
to make his father proud.

DEAR AZULA,

Avatar: The Last Airbender

The lesson my mother taught me was,

finish the job.

When her's could not be finished,
I forged myself into a prodigy.

I propped my girl vessel
atop my ash throne. Lead the empire
of play house; its empty cupboards and
silent rooms

kneaded shadows behind
shut-tight doors. Azula, I wanted your

power. I wanted a hunger yielding
lightning. A crown never corroded by

silence.

I beat my brother to being the favorite child:

When opportunity came,
I didn't wait for softness.

Finish the job.

I puppet for power.
But I, too, am just a kindling
kind of girl.

I, too, have pulverized the mirror
in the quiet of my bedroom
and demanded of a lineage

to just love me
enough

that I wouldn't
have to be

this
cruel.

BLACK FIRE BALLAD
(I FEEL MOST EVIL IN MY MOTHER'S GOWNS)
Teen Titans

I know I make you sick. Sister,
some strange planet
we left behind. War cry,
my lullaby. Our exploded mother,
shaking inside me. Some strange planets
I go to for mercy—a stranger's mouth,
a mystery, to lick the salt from sorrow.
I burn what won't be burned. I go dark
for days. Why won't you love me
this way?

●

I say *mother* / but it comes out / *suffer/*
there's a bug/ in my downloaded / diva/
my bootleg / femme / fatale / failure / I
was eight / I was twelve / nineteen /
twenty when you saw / me / wearing our
mom / you've seen / who / I'm trying to
be / and say / nothing / why do I keep /
failing? / I say / *mother* / but I come out
/

monster.

●

Because I'll never be beautiful, not really,
I dress myself in weapons:
laser, adder, stiletto, smoke.
I build myself bigger, six inch
heel through an adam's apple.
I take a bite.

I take a life.
Some sad boy calls me
kitty-cat. I crack
my neck, and wet my nails
in his red. Don't
touch me.
I am not the pretty sister, I am
the bitch who wins.
There's not a boy or beast
who can look at me and live.
Not even the one I used to be.

•

I don't mean
to be cruel
but, like blister
beetles, like honey
bees I must be
aposematic.
My softness
coated in acrylic,
armor, allure.
My whole life
someone told me
to be a weapon,
when all I wanted
was to weep.

FIONA CHOSE TO BE AN OGRE
Shrek

*"Fiona chose to be an ogre over being a white woman. What
does that tell you?"*   —Luther Hughes, Twitter

"How rude it is to exist when no one wants you."
         —Lord Farquad

I used to chase princes
who wanted nothing
to do with me.

On the blacktop in third grade,
my body wrapped around
my white crush's ankles after
he tried to fight me.

I was his princess, if
I could convince him I was worth saving.

Teeth-feathered boa, copper consolation crown,
sick suitor, muddied elementary gown.

The moments it took him to shake me off
I called

devotion. With later suitors,

I slept with my face against
the wall. I locked myself
in the bathroom and spent hours
tracing my nose in the mirror,

sloughing off my olive hide
for the princess I thought was submerged
underneath.

When my prince stomped on my naked head,
it must have been because his care was too clumsy.
Maybe he would chase me

if I was a white girl;
I wouldn't be his monster.

I must be cursed out the crown
femininity promised me.

I stayed up years waiting
to be told I was beautiful. I fought

my mirror, my prince
and lost, and lost, and lost

myself till glory emerged. I made
myself sick, so sick

I became a fever pitch.
Not pretty enough for mercy, yet
I have always been true love's form.
Whiteness was too scared to rescue

my ugly. My ugly is mine, sickening.
I am the type of brown stunning that crushes
her captives. Every white girl wants

a piece of me. My plaster crown,
my soil kingdom. My teeth,
glinting rude ore.

I am a girl searching for her savagery,
even when it's doomed.

I am the color of envy,
and my suitor loves it, too.

REFRACTION

Mulan

Mama said I looked like
her daughter in the dresses she
bought to redeem me. She swaddled
my powdered face, my refined
mirrors. I weave my refractions,
quarter their collateral dreams in my empty
daughter fate. I lose my face defending
home. This pageantry is to protect me from
donning my war gown. Too treacherous
hares run side by side. *How can you tell*
If I am she?

a boy with half my head shaved.
clotted with gauze and taffeta
transgression. Red rogue
sword. I am a wish rattled between two
armors. I matricide her old clothes,
closet deserted. Still, I am no perfect
butch. I don't hear Mama calling me
the soldier I'm becoming. In my reflection I'm
at home in the war of my making. Free
if I am he or

MURDER BALLAD, RAVEN: PATRICIDE

From Teen Titans

Because I'm nothing like my father,
I give him the grace of burial. One plot

for his body. Another to plant
his donkey head

though I sawed the antlers off.
Wouldn't I be a better girl if he knew

this kind of mercy? The chance
to become an offering, a seed

that bears more seeds. One day
his carcass will break

the soil. Another lesson in light.
What did he teach?

Everything my father gave me
goes dark. Even me.

My father's sour blood-jewel.

Every man is an apocalypse. So what
of their daughters?

Our inheritance?
Are we born to clean their wars?

To lick iron where they open?
I do not believe in any prophecy,

except the ones I wrote.
I close

the coffin
of his jaw.

Nothing grows
from there. This is how

the spell ends:
goat hoof, grackle, the eyes

of my spider goddess
clicking shut.

YZMA DRESSES FOR THE LLAMA FUNERAL

The Emperor's New Groove

> *"a man has always wanted to lay me down,*
> *but he never wanted to pick me up" —Eartha*
> *Kitt, on the Terry Wogan Show, 1989*

In the laboratory I scheme
elaborately what I will wear
to the pyre of the boy I am
trying to kill. How I would look
with his fluted spine
slung around my neck
like a mink. I prefer fur
or snake hide. Poison
in a chalice, his plasma
curdled green. I'll take a sip,
then slip into my second skin-
tight fit: a patent leather lab coat.
Dissect his gullied stomach.
Glamour, my guardian.
Seduction, my scalpel.
What treasures will I find
when I gut the man
standing in my place?
My final ingredients,
the last piece of alchemy
I need to shapeshift
into royalty. I hope I don't
become him. Brutal
ruler, blood glut, his line of concubines,
a need to own: land, water, bodies,
the ugly ornaments of a boy king.
I know, I need beauty to topple
awful gods, men
who think they own me.
But what will I be

when the venom settles?
At my coronation, will I wear
my evening gown?
Or will I keep his clothes?
Red robe, headdress,
his ugly cloud of musk.

BEAST/BOY

Teen Titans

I came from the forest wet, red. I sprouted
gills and crossed three rivers. In the night
I wove silk webs. I am every beast that catches my eye.
Rams burst from my back, glottal and bleating.
Serpents slip my throat like silver ribbons.

We came from creatures slick-skinned and yellow-eyed,
so I shapeshift by mapping my bloodline. Even the insects
and I are tied by generations. I know all species
by name. I call the trees my kin.
Whoever trespasses the animal kingdom trespasses me.

You think me cruel. What scares you more,
the venom or the beak? What you hear or what you see?
You make me rich with fear.When I close my twenty eyes,
the faces that haunt me are your kind:
CEOs who boiled rivers cheap, sharkskin oligarchy,
investors, wealthy men with skin so white it glows.
Meat.

Bring me the man who paid for this apocalypse,
and I will teach him what it means to be a beast.
In the ring of fire I will dare him to say my name,
watch as I assume his form. His hand on his throat.
His eye watching his eye. I am just the mirror
violence passes through. Ancestors of night caw

and red beak, make me as wicked as this one,
who ignites his house with the family inside.
Make me a creature who always survives.

MARROW
(FOR THE HYENAS)
The Lion King

Do you know what we do to kings who step out their kingdom? /
We laugh / They pin our throats to the dirt / and look damn ugly
/ doing it / We erupt into hysteria / hysteria a coup / where light
does not / have the guts to touch / We thrive / We laugh the
gallows / inside out / They ask me / *how hard is it to be born*
hyena? / I say / *I hit the jackpot* / I say / Our feast of marrow is
sweet / and long / We live / to inherit a scorned kingdom / We
sing / in our graveyard / Our dead stay in good company / Our
kings live only as long as

our appetites / The world teeters / on our haunches when we
shudder / and dance / We laugh and this scares you / We are
loyal only to our joy / feral / this scares you /

We eat your kings and this is Black / our grin / guillotine / this
is Black / this is Black /

this is still Black.

ZUKO'S PALINODE

Avatar: The Last Airbender

Iroh,

You taught me fire is also good
for making tea.

You taught me dragon's breath
smells like jasmine.

Bend the lightning back into the clouds;
I have no use for murder.

Oh candlewick. Oh little heartbeat.

> *Pride is not the opposite of shame,*
> *but its source.*

What happens to the boys who burn
ourselves down? Is that where we find
the softest part?

I watched my brother pluck loquats
in the garden, gold flesh pulsing in his palm.

I hope he knows he's beautiful.
Oh honor. Fuck honor.
Who made you king of kings?

Was it the myths we wrote of men?
Was it father? Is he dead too? Is he laid with ugly
grief? Did he inherit it from his?
Did he kill it in the flame?

I am not reverent at the altar
where he offered me anymore.

Every fire must go out.
You taught me that.

Oh Iroh. Oh Uncle.
You are the only fire master
as gentle as the ocean.

My burns cool in your soft light
your big-bellied glow.

I learned love
in the steam

rising from your tea.

DEAR AZULA, FAREWELL

Avatar: The Last Airbender

The last time I left home, my mother cried
at the foot of the stairs and said,
it gets harder every time.

Our scars are not sexy or ceremonial.

In the lonely of our bedrooms
after our rejection, we
unclog our hairbrushes
of glass. We think
we do this alone,

while our mothers
wait on us to open
the door.

The story still wants a villain.

But we are not monsters,
we are girls gnawing for the love
we believed a throne would break
for us.

I love you, I do.
I am not afraid of you anymore.

MY MOM AND MRS. INCREDIBLE HAVE THE SAME HAIRCUT
The Incredibles

Light red, manageable length, something between soccer mom and "can I speak to the manager?" They could be wine aunties together. Gal pals who buy each other pillow cases from Etsy that say "it's wine time!" or "mom's sippy cup" with a picture of a spilling glass. Always red. Who comment on each other's Facebook posts with heart-eye emojis. "Look how grown he is!" my mother will comment on a video of Dash breaking the sound barrier. "So blessed!" Mrs. Incredible will say below a photo of my little sister playing cello, last chair.

They will spend eternity driving their kids to practices and performances and missions to save the world. They will make their children's report cards and blue ribbons into monuments. They will never sleep, and pretend it's fine. Who are these white-toothed women? And where do they put their grief? When I was little, my mom used to take long car rides, just to get away. Sometimes, she'd take me with her. Sometimes, she'd go alone. The car was always quiet as her eyes. Even with the radio on, I could tell there was no sound inside her.

I want to make my mother proud. I want to massage her spine. I know that I will never know what my mother does to keep me safe, but I keep trying to make it up. How thin do we stretch her? My siblings and I, do we love her right? Did we ever ask? Even while I'm away at college she always texts: *call me, call me, I just want to reach you.*

MY GIRLFRIEND TURNS INTO THE MOON

Avatar: The Last Airbender

I whisper your name to make sure I can still say it,
a lacquered prayer not lost to the waning moon.

When we were snowed in last winter, you held me between your
palms and drank lunar tea. Laughing, we sipped to empty the moon.

When I was in love, dawn came too quickly. Every night a trophy
offering. Crafted each other, deities. We loved under the still moon.

Someone small and wavering lives in the missing of you. Cleaves
memory through sand. Finds a force to blame: time, moon.

We're done. The best and the worst of you compete for legend.
I leave icons at the foot of nostalgia. We look up at the same moon.

Let us love our growth and our memory, Azura. Savor the loss.
Thank all the phases under the waxing moon.

ACKNOWLEDGEMENTS

"Making art with someone is the most intimate thing you can do."
—*First Wave Parable*

Azura, I sent you one text, and you said *yes*. I am honored to call you my friend, my tenderness, my co-creator. I don't know that I would have been brave enough to say what must be said if you weren't by my side. Thank you, for sharing the page with me. I don't know what could be closer.

Jackson, you asked, "wanna do something crazy?" and I said yes. I didn't even need to know what it was in the moment. I am so grateful for our trust, for your luminary mind, for the late nights and being in this journey with you. I love you so much.

Thank you Tanesha, Safia, and the entire Button Team for believing in our dream.

For Gretchen, Sofía, Chis, James, Gia, Tommy. For 12thCo WealthCo. For Lucky 13th. We are, First Wave.

For Meta-Four Houston, Bean, D.E.E.P., Loyce, Patricia, Elizabeth, Angela and everyone at WITS Houston. My teammates: Adam, Lynn, Rukmini, Carl, Oasis, Sunny, Jadon, Shunn, Sebastian, even you Donald. For Write About Now, CoogSlam, and all the poets in Houston. Aris, Muhammad, Jazzib, Kenny, Wasiq, RJ. Y'all keep my pockets full of poems.

For the girls: Aidan, Alex, Zack, and the rest of y'all. You teach me about the woman I want to be.

Gratitude always for my Youth Speaks Seattle family. My mentors and dearest homies Will Giles, Ebo Barton, Christina Nguyen, all my teammates. And my Babel Poetry family for being there at this project's inception.

And to my twelve year old self, I know you're proud of me for still writing fanfiction.

NOTES

The concept of "a game we made ourselves" in *Zuko's Ode* is borrowed from Aidan Forster.

The line "I am a girl searching for her savagery, even when it's doomed" is taken from June Jordan's *Poem for Nana*.

The line "how can you tell if I am he or if I am she?" is a translated excerpt from *The Ballad of Mulan*.

"I hit the jackpot" in *Marrow* is a quote from James Baldwin in the film, "The Price of the Ticket" (1989) dir. Karen Thorsen and Doug Dempsey.

The line "pride is not the opposite of shame,/ but its source" in *Zuko's Palinode* is a quote by the character Uncle Iroh in the tv show, *Avatar: The Last Airbender*.

The line, "Your father is only your father/ until one of you forgets" in *Zuko's Palinode* is from Ocean Vuong's poem, *Someday I'll Love Ocean Vuong*.

"I love you, I do" in *Dear Azula, Farewell* is a direct quote from Azula's mother in *Avatar: The Last Airbender*.

ABOUT THE AUTHOR

Jackson Neal (He/They) is a poet from Houston, Texas. They are the 2019 National Youth Poet Laureate Ambassador for the Southwest and the 2019 Houston Youth Poet Laureate. Neal is a First Wave Scholar at the University of Wisconsin-Madison where they are pursuing a dual BFA in English, Creative Writing and Dance. Follow their work at jacksonneal.com, or @jaxnealpoetry on Twitter and Instagram.

ABOUT THE AUTHOR

Azura Tyabji served as the 2018-19 Seattle Youth Poet Laureate and National Youth Poet Ambassador for the West region. Her debut poetry collection, Stepwell, was released by Poetry Northwest in 2018. She is currently a First Wave scholar studying Sociology and English, Creative Writing at the University of Wisconsin-Madison. She can be found @azura.tyabji on Instagram and Twitter.

OTHER BOOKS BY BUTTON POETRY

If you enjoyed this book, please consider checking out
some of our others, below. Readers like you allow us
to keep broadcasting and publishing. Thank you!

Neil Hilborn, *Our Numbered Days*
Hanif Abdurraqib, *The Crown Ain't Worth Much*
Sabrina Benaim, *Depression & Other Magic Tricks*
Rudy Francisco, *Helium*
Rachel Wiley, *Nothing Is Okay*
Neil Hilborn, *The Future*
Phil Kaye, *Date & Time*
Andrea Gibson, *Lord of the Butterflies*
Blythe Baird, *If My Body Could Speak*
Desireé Dallagiacomo, *SINK*
Dave Harris, *Patricide*
Michael Lee, *The Only Worlds We Know*
Raych Jackson, *Even the Saints Audition*
Brenna Twohy, *Swallowtail*
Porsha Olayiwola, *i shimmer sometimes, too*
Jared Singer, *Forgive Yourself These Tiny Acts of Self-Destruction*
Adam Falkner, *The Willies*
Kerrin McCadden, *Keep This To Yourself*
George Abraham, *Birthright*
Omar Holmon, *We Were All Someone Else Yesterday*
Rachel Wiley, *Fat Girl Finishing School*
Nava EtShalom, *Fortunately*
Bianca Phipps, *crown noble*
Rudy Francisco, *I'll Fly Away*
Natasha T. Miller, *Butcher*
Kevin Kantor, *Please Come Off-Book*
Ollie Schminkey, *Dead Dad Jokes*

Available at buttonpoetry.com/shop and more!